THE CRYPTO REVOLUTION

THE CRYPTO REVOLUTION

CARMEN WILDE

CONTENTS

1. Introduction — 1
2. Understanding Cryptocurrencies — 3
3. Blockchain Technology — 9
4. Investing in Cryptocurrencies — 13
5. Regulation and Compliance — 17
6. Cryptocurrency Exchanges — 19
7. Security and Wallets — 23
8. Cryptocurrency Mining — 27
9. Emerging Trends in Cryptocurrencies — 31
10. The Future of Cryptocurrencies — 35
11. Conclusion — 39

Copyright © 2024 by Carmen Wilde
All rights reserved. No part of this book may be reproduced in any manner whatsoever without written permission except in the case of brief quotations embodied in critical articles and reviews.
First Printing, 2024

CHAPTER 1

Introduction

What is the future of money? Unlike with other revolutionary inventions such as the telephone, electricity, and paper money, many today cannot frame an image of tomorrow's money. Who will be the Bell, Tesla, or Ben Franklin of monetary innovation? Slowly over time, barter systems evolved into ever more efficient exchanges. Shells, leather, tobacco, and a myriad of other commodities were used as money along the way. Eventually, precious metal coins were cast and their value - the metal content - certified by a central authority. Barter became easier and inefficiencies reduced.

Moving metal coins was difficult and theft was rampant. As a solution, central institutions arose to certify money deposits and to provide safe custody. Paper claims substituting for metal money on deposit multiplied, and medieval banks magnified the amount of money in circulation through fractional lending. Then the central certified coins were abandoned and only paper banknotes remained. As our paper money is irredeemable, our money today is fiat money - valid only because the government says it is. Yet central institutions have relapsed on their monopoly to issue fiat money, and a fissure in the very nature of money has emerged. Welcome to the crypto revolution.

CHAPTER 2

Understanding Cryptocurrencies

Cryptocurrencies are all the rage right now. It seems that you can't go anywhere without hearing someone talking about buying or selling cryptocurrencies - whether it be Bitcoin, Ethereum, or countless other cryptocurrencies that are out there today. But what exactly is a "cryptocurrency", and what does our growing interest in them say about the society in which we live? In this chapter, we will shine some light on the intersection of economics and technology that cryptocurrency embodies. For a bit of grounding, we will tip our hats to the conceptualizations of money and the digital economy that have come before the rise of cryptocurrency. We will touch on some fundamental aspects of how cryptocurrency functions; and finally, we will explore both the rise of blockchain technology and the rise of the tremendous interest in anything that models or utilizes it. After reading this chapter, you should understand why the rise of cryptocurrencies is a significant event within society today.

Points: 1. The Core Addresses the Digital Economy at the Nexus of Economics and Technology. 2. Money Defined. 3. Today's Money. 4. Problems with Today's Money. 5. The Digital Economy:

The Emergence of Finance and Technology. 6. FinTech and Its Impact Today. 7. What is Cryptocurrency? 8. How Cryptocurrency Works. 9. The Rise of Bitcoin. 10. Bitcoin's Disruption. 11. Bitcoin's Future. 12. Models of Bitcoin. 13. The Takeaway.

Definition and History

The Bitcoin peer-to-peer network, which uses modern cryptography, achieves the function of a central bank in a distributed way, verifies all transactions across the network, and records the amount of Bitcoin circulating in the blockchain database, and issues predetermined total Bitcoin completion rules. Achieves financial security. Bitcoin creates a mathematical cryptocurrency and achieves both double spend attacks and Byzantine failures. The key component of Bitcoin is a special digital signature and public key using the modern best practice signature ECDSA. In 1990, Japanese computer scientist Hashimoto proposed the concept of a public key digital signature, which has since been widely used and continues to be popular until the ECDSA signature technology is created. The ECDSA implementation does not require complex calculations and achieves the performance improvements of hundreds or even thousands of times, minimizes the complexity of the protocol, and achieves higher security performance and emphasizes the advantage of Badelta.

Bitcoin is a mathematically scarce digital currency that operates on decentralized networks of computers. It eliminates the need for third-party financial institutions and allows proportional participation in its network by facilitating democratic financial access to the unbanked. In traditional money, money has historically been based on either metals and minerals or politics and can be lost due to fire, water, theft, etc., and it takes a long time to move. The modern concept of a dollar in my hand originated from a burning receipt. Unlike traditional money, money such as virtual currency and digital currency, which is proposed as an alternative to traditional money, has appeared. The value of digital terrain is valued at zero before the emergence of Bitcoin, which is a virtual digital currency, and after it is proven by Bitcoin and has opened new executives to challenge the established currency order, the virtual economy has once again become the focus of the world. On January 3, 2009, Nakamoto created and distributed the first Bitcoin software to create digital currency with privacy and security, and the distributed network operated automatically.

Key Features

Should Bitcoin's limitations be removed or mitigated, it is generally very suitable as a candidate for a new world reserve currency. Since its inception, it has become one in terms of media attention at least. Nonetheless, the search for an explanation about what the role of Bitcoin in the international monetary system of the future would be has remained inconclusive.

Globality. Bitcoin is the first form of money that is natively constructed to be globally used. Being digital. Digital characteristics are advantageous over current forms of money, providing a) enhanced security, b) extremely fast transaction confirmations, c) near real-time record keeping, d) always-available accounting records, and also e) being suitable for high-frequency trading. Transferring Bitcoin is immune to error and irreversible because there are no counterfeit risks when the bitcoin is not in someone's custody. Ease to divide, combine, and reconcile. A feature named divisibility allows for micropayments and usage of otherwise non-standard denominations. Further, "colored coin" tokens can be imitated by bulk-dividing Bitcoin money and will allow for new financial creative, security-exchangeable forms of Bitcoin.

As argued by Demeester (2015), Bitcoin is an emergent monetary system that might create a new financial world order. Bitcoin has several key features that make it suitable for several specialized cases, allows for extremely valuable financial applications, and can greatly enhance the function of money. This suggests that, despite most misunderstandings that exist in developed markets, Bitcoin indeed has highly desirable use cases. A list of these specific features includes:

Types of Cryptocurrencies

First, it is necessary to distinguish between a cryptocurrency and a crypto asset. While we use the names interchangeably sometimes, they're not quite the same. In general, a cryptocurrency is a digital token and is used specifically as a medium of exchange. That is, we use a cryptocurrency to make transactions. The difference between a cryptocurrency and digital cash like Venmo or PayPal is the fact that a cryptocurrency contains a very specific built-in protected accounting system with a secure ledger that ensures it can't be double spent. PayPal transactions, on the other hand, are so closely and automatically reconciled against the existing Litecoin that it's almost impossible to come up with any inconsistency in the names provided we trust PayPal to have a reliable internal reconciliation process. The same is not true for a cryptocurrency, which is supposed to provide a trustless environment to minimize the influence of intermediaries on economic and financial transactions.

In the case of cryptocurrencies, their first use case, though the original intention was much wider, is often regarded as a store of value. Like everything else, however, this new technology is not homogeneous. There are a variety of ways to differentiate one coin or token from another. And while we continue to learn about the tokens, it's important to have a basic understanding of some of the crypto landscape's recognizable features.

The initial and most exciting use case for a new technology often generates tremendous enthusiasm. That's certainly the case for things like the World Wide Web in the 1990s, the American automobile industry in the early 20th century, or, in the 1880s, my favorite, the creation of the electric utility ecosystem.

CHAPTER 3

Blockchain Technology

In exploratory financial situations like the blockchain, technology choices by society tend to go into cycles. For example, the Internet bubble in the 1990s didn't deliver the expected new technological advances, but ultimately it led to massive investments being made in broadband and fiber-optics in the early 2000s that eventually completed 25 years of allowing some bits to travel cheaper and others more expensive. Bold technological moves - the point of the bubbles - therefore left the technology track in the background. We will track the blockchain idea as it goes through this financial bubble when we try to focus on the technologies that could bring into being fundamentally different technological designs, specifically to the blockchain.

Blockchain technology is best understood as a critical innovation that enabled the birth and growth of Bitcoin. Bitcoin was the first 'killer app' of blockchain. From the time it was first deployed in January 2009, it has managed to gain an expansive user base of people who use it for anything from an ordinary currency to a speculative investor's view of the future of finance. Others may use Bitcoin for completely new applications, since it forms part of sophisticated technological systems - the blockchain - that were not designed to operate only as internet money. Bitcoin is fundamentally a software codebase. It appears to us that Bitcoin has managed to become a standard of money, perhaps for the time it has lasted, but that the blockchain technology offers likely alternative paths.

What is Blockchain?

According to the first keepers, "each block contains a cryptographic hash of the previous block, a timestamp and the transaction data". Any changes to previous blocks to the data stored in them will make the current block point to a different one and can be easily spotted by the network, actively blocking in such manner the possibility of accomplishing the desired of modifying the registry and distributing the messages, with various factors asymmetrically disturbing the activity or revealing suspicion through various data extraction methods, such as clustering and classification.

The idea of blockchain was first introduced around 1992 with the idea of securing a digital archive. Thanks to some unique properties, among them transparency and security, some people thought of extending its uses even further. While we can have a private blockchain, one that doesn't need the internet, this transparency is what allows a blockchain to change the way we interact and offer a service, independently of the first people behind the simple idea of securing an archive or digital money. There are currently hundreds of working ideas and thousands of proofs of concept. But what, again, is blockchain? A blockchain is, in the most ordinary description possible, a chain containing blocks. Each block consists of a series of transactions - paychecks, certificate approves, smaller monetary transactions - confirmed by a network of online users. Once that block is full, a new block is created.

How Does Blockchain Work?

The thousands of nodes connected to a blockchain are all keeping track of the same chain. That is significant. If a hacker wanted to change a single entry in the blockchain, they would have to hack into every single node in the entire network and change the entire chain. That would require more computational power than the entire network combined. Moreover, if a hacker changes a single entry in a chain on even one block, that block would have to be replicated throughout the network; but it couldn't be because the chain wouldn't be the same on every single node. So, even if all this computational power was available, the hacker would not be able to replicate every single block that was changed. The network would see the attempted change and immediately identify it as a hack and refuse to allow the altered chain to be added to the network. Assuming it were possible for a patient hacker or group of hackers to change every single block in a blockchain, once a block was modified, it would have to be accepted as the correct chain throughout the network. Since a consensus among the majority of chains in the network is required to verify a blockchain, an altered chain that was out of sync with the rest of the network would be quickly and easily identified.

Applications of Blockchain

If the blockchain enthusiasts of the world are successful, this is what they are going to look like: the future will be filled with invisible infrastructure," says Erick Miller, CEO of CoinCircle. "New and modernized rails that will move money and assets with less friction, reduced cost to end users, and instantaneous settlement. Blockchain technology allows us to not just make transactions, by creating secure and instantaneous movement of money and assets between parties, but it can revolutionize scores of financial products insurance, lending, nonbank-issued ATMs, and more. But the real revolution will be in things we can't imagine Buyer-to-seller product attribute matching. Fast, simple electronic ownership transfers for anything eXtensible Business Reporting Language (XBRL). The big picture is that blockchain technology offers startups and existing financial service corporations new ways to create value. Building these places is the next great opportunity.

Applying blockchain technology to existing business problems might reduce the number of solutions that fail because they aren't integrated into existing systems. For example, it's often difficult to get a company to install an entirely new authentication system even when it has a quick payback period. But a new system that uses micropayments to create a "self-authenticating" capability might have a quicker user-acceptance curve. Another common failure problem related to blockchain technology is the tendency to go overboard on blockchainization. Not every company is looking for world domination. Not every idea is going to change our lives. Now that's hard-nosed realism. If you are just looking for a faster way to send pennies between New York, London, and Luxembourg, you're not going to change the world.

CHAPTER 4

Investing in Cryptocurrencies

When speaking about cryptos, though, it is of utmost importance to separate the issue of digital coins from that of assets. Cryptocurrencies are to be viewed as a genuine new form of money in that they are mainly used for making payments in day-to-day transactions. Non-financial corporations, which are the first corporate driver in the cryptocurrency listings, but also consumers invest in cryptocurrencies as a form of "virtual wallet"; or, even more often, they receive these digital coins as a consideration for sales of goods, services, and property.

Investors looking for opportunities to benefit from the ongoing crypto revolution have various options, including buying cryptocurrencies outright, investing in cryptocurrency derivatives, investing in cryptocurrency mining, and investing in companies that are related to cryptocurrencies. Cryptocurrencies, or cryptos for short, are directly investable. For those wanting to invest in the future of money, cryptos represent the easiest, most direct way to do it. The reasons why anyone can now invest in this asset class by buying directly are that, first, there are plenty of ways to gain access to them; second, there are multiple marketplaces; and third, they are easy to handle.

Cryptos can be accessed over the internet through marketplaces and kept in virtual wallets which are designed specifically for this purpose.

Benefits and Risks

We would never advocate for all assets to be held in digital assets. Rather, it is complementary to a personal or institutional investment portfolio that is typically comprised of a variety of different asset classes such as stocks, bonds, real estate, currencies, equities, commodities, and so on. It is our belief that the prudent addition of diversified digital assets to a well-constructed portfolio can complement existing asset classes and add even further diversification to a financial portfolio. Wealth preservation, long-term value, privacy, censorship, and confiscation resistance are all values that appeal to many crypto holders and are reasons why integration can be a thoughtful and rewarding addition.

It is important to carefully consider not only the long-term value of any investments, but especially the short-term risks because digital assets such as cryptocurrencies have had extreme volatility and drawdowns. Investors must be able and willing to withstand dramatic price swings that can result in severe reductions in capital, not compliant with the general goals of preservation of capital, income, and appreciation. Furthermore, investing in digital assets carries with it unique risks that investments of the same magnitude in assets such as US dollars, deposit accounts, or indexed exchange-traded funds do not.

Strategies for Investing

Traders who have experience buying and selling stocks on the stock exchange are advised not to transfer these skills directly to the digital currency world. Instead, they should spend time observing and learning how the market moves and how digital currencies function. While momentum traders subject to strong winds can make substantial profits in a short period of time, they can just as easily lose money with the same but more volatile returns. With such strong momentum moves, the purchase of a digital currency could require a level of comfort that makes one acceptable for a wild, unregulated roller coaster ride. Users are encouraged to seriously consider the financial and mental capacity to assume this type of responsibility before making any commitment.

The bottom line is that a buy-and-hold strategy will reward all who are patient. This isn't to say that one shouldn't be open to trading out of certain positions, especially if a person who buys a percentage of crypto assets on the stock exchange lists new assets. However, the reality is that it's almost impossible to consistently predict the winners in the digital currency world. The easiest and most mentally relaxing strategy is to build a portfolio based on fixed income, market capitalization, and scientific criteria, and commit to holding each asset for a longer period of time – say, from several years to at least ten years.

CHAPTER 5

Regulation and Compliance

The U.S. government has reacted to the proponents of ICOs and the use of cryptocurrencies to conduct business as if they believe they operate in an error-free environment. This is the polar opposite of how the U.S. Securities and Exchange Commission (SEC) mandates that it requires excessive information to be provided to potential investors. The SEC believes the source of the money should not be used to judge potential investments. As the SEC, led by a championship chess player, continues to investigate, it is likely that they will levy fines for fraud on most companies that did not adhere to SEC regulations with their ICO. The majority of the $6B+ that was raised by the 1600+ ICOs will significantly decrease. If the SEC were to require new regulations where extensive information and licensing was required for both individual ICO buyers as well as the companies that are conducting ICOs, this would inhibit the SEC's ability to generate revenue without any fiduciary restrictions being extended to ICO buyers. The use of blockchain technology has presented new problems that require immediate attention. Countries that are proactive and create regulatory environments that are investor-friendly will attract the most talented developers and will also maximize their ability to capture the value. Countries that mishandle the intersection of blockchain technology and investor protection will cause companies to relocate to other countries and increase the level of crypto-related fraud.

Cryptocurrencies and Initial Coin Offerings (ICOs) are relatively new and highly disruptive to traditional finance systems. How should these financial innovations be regulated to ensure they are not used for illicit purposes, such as money laundering or financing terrorism, or for committing fraud? This is a difficult and polarizing issue. The issue of how governments will tax and manage the vast amounts of wealth created by those who invested in cryptocurrencies or ICOs is another problem the current regulatory systems are struggling to solve.

CHAPTER 6

Cryptocurrency Exchanges

The ripple effect on price and the top 10 cryptocurrencies was like a Western bar where the first one who started the brawl was the only one to win. Nonetheless, with its bad management, it still affected the reputation of other exchanges. The collapse prompted many millionaire businesses to consider whether cryptocurrency should be legal due to alleged money laundering or to fight piracy. At the hearing, politicians asked many questions that are common today, and more evidence was given that proved private and public blockchains have the same vulnerabilities and advantages as data storage techniques. At the same hearing, the FBI testified the following: "The criminal is quick to jump on a new and developing communication system. We have wiretapped telephones, looked at internet chat rooms, and the criminal is quick to adapt. We will see that with this newish/ developing technology called bitcoin. Let's not forget, the more we execute methods to take on the internet, the more the criminal jumps to stay ahead of us, and the same has been demonstrated by our previous testimony".

In 2013, there were very few exchanges. When Mt. Gox, the leading exchange at the time, collapsed, it suffered the fate of many startups: it couldn't handle the problems associated with rapid growth. The surge of interest in cryptocurrency took it by surprise - it was a victim of its own success. It wasn't equipped to handle the cyber-attacks that followed. It was hit by distributed denial of service (DDoS), which occurred during December 2013, when the price of bitcoin skyrocketed from $200 to $1,000. This happened without Satoshi releasing this technology, leaving it only as just a white paper. Critics started pointing fingers saying bitcoin was a speculative bubble, applying Ben's theory. Larger investors who traded at Mt. Gox went to their preferred medium (the news media) and started fueling panic. In the panic that ensued and its widespread coverage, the price collapsed, leaving traders unable to trade due to DDoS.

Types of Exchanges

Now that you understand the types of exchanges you can use to buy and sell cryptocurrencies, let's go over the main types of exchanges you will come across.

Peer-to-Peer Platforms: These are websites that act as intermediaries between people looking to buy and sell cryptocurrencies. When you buy from P2P networks, you are actually buying directly from another person. This being the case, price discovery can be a bit of a challenge because the price you agree to can fluctuate depending on who you are dealing with. But that is part of the whole negotiation process. On P2P platforms, the buyer usually selects from a list of best offers based on pricing, payment method, and seller feedback. The latter is crucial because the platform needs to demonstrate to the buyer who they are dealing with, improving the chances of successful trade completion.

Decentralized Exchanges: A decentralized exchange (DEX) is an exchange market that does not rely on a third-party service to hold the customer's funds. Instead, a DEX operates at the blockchain level, so trades don't need to be regulated by an intermediary. Peer-to-peer and box-type exchanges are popular features, but there shouldn't really be any limitations to the kind of buy and sell orders available on a DEX. Participants on a DEX communicate directly with each other, provide liquidity to the market, and control their own private keys. All cryptocurrencies, therefore, should be able to trade on DEX, subject to wallet availability. Since there is no authority, the rates are fixed by the market itself. At the time of writing, liquidity is an issue, with a lot of new DEX entries popping up over the last twelve months, most of which do not have large trade volumes.

Centralized Exchanges: The most common way to buy Bitcoin, Ethereum, or any other cryptocurrency is to use a centralized exchange. However, this type of exchange is not as simple as it sounds. Every transaction that takes place has rules and principles that should be followed. The fact a purchase or sale takes place on an exchange doesn't mean investors have access to some kind of assets. Instead, if investors want to withdraw their assets, this usually translates to a second transaction, which ultimately may give them access to the assets acquired. The complex legal framework exists to regulate operations and which cryptocurrencies are to be withdrawn. On exchanges, trades are typically maintained as a record between parties. The exchange is responsible for adding new funds and withdrawing the equivalent value of the transaction to the trading platform. These trades are often carried out very quickly and involve professional traders.

Choosing the Right Exchange

Once you decide to buy Bitcoins, you should store them in a wallet that is separate from the exchange you used. Online wallets in particular are vulnerable to hacking, so you should have physical possession of the coins you own. Software like Electrum, Dark Wallet, and Multibit allow you to keep full control of your digital Bitcoin wallet on your computer, so even if your exchange or online wallet is fraudulent, hacked, or shut down, the coins are still in your possession. Keeping your wallet on your computer is also the first step towards using the Bitcoin network as a secure bank. Remember, there are no intermediaries in your financial transactions, so you should consider yourself your own bank. The security of your bank is only as secure as you keep your online presence. Protect your Bitcoins in the same way you would secure your bank account. With Bitcoin, you have the power to control your financial future, so learn how to use it wisely and thoughtfully.

Bitcoin is global and open, so you can use any Bitcoin exchange, anywhere in the world. To exchange dollars for Bitcoins, you can use any reputable exchange service. Some of the most popular exchanges include Coinbase, BitStamp, Btc-e, Coinsetter, and Itbit. You open an account and link it to your home bank account. After a few days, you can wire transfer money to the exchange and use the money to buy Bitcoins at the market price. The exchange will act as a custodian for the Bitcoins you buy until you decide to do something with them. You can also exchange dollars for Bitcoins using services like BitInstant and BitPay, which link directly to your bank account, but these services are less regulated and not meant for individuals who are unfamiliar with dealing with Bitcoin. You can also exchange currency for Bitcoins directly with other individuals using peer-to-peer exchanges such as LocalBitcoins or BitQuick. The upside is that you get access to Bitcoins faster and avoid the registration and account funding process. The downside is that you take on much higher counterparty and fraud risk, and you may end up overpaying for the coins if the service sets an unfavorable exchange rate.

CHAPTER 7

Security and Wallets

While the cryptocurrency space as a whole is growing and becoming more secure by the day, there are a number of warnings that should be highlighted before you rush out and start buying popular cryptocurrencies like Bitcoin and Ethereum. Security is a critical aspect in the world of cryptocurrency, and the internet is filled with stories of people getting messed up. It is of utmost importance that you invest responsibly and use security best practices while participating in this financial revolution. Unlike traditional financial institutions that have safety nets and can help recover your funds if something does go wrong, there are no third parties that can grant your account access or reverse a transaction. This means that you need to be very mindful of what is going on with your funds at all times.

The crypto revolution: Investing in the future of money will go into great depth about the most disruptive technology to come around in a long time. Cryptocurrency and blockchain technology can be extremely complex, and for all the benefits that cryptocurrency offers to society, it is not readily accessible to those who are not technologically savvy. Furthermore, cryptocurrency can be a confusing topic, which is both easy to get hacked in and easy to lose funds forever. To address many of these issues, this chapter will provide a series of resources to avoid possible catastrophes associated with cryptocurrency.

Types of Wallets
Hot Wallets

A hot wallet refers to a Bitcoin wallet that is connected to the internet. Hot wallets are the most common way to store Bitcoin and are generally more accessible than a cold wallet. As the funds are placed online, it introduces the risks of hacking to your Bitcoin. Despite the increased risk, hot wallets are the most common choice as they provide easier access to Bitcoin and are easy to use. The most common type of hot wallet is a software wallet. Just like its name, this kind of wallet is designed as an app or a software program that can be installed on mobile phones or computers. Web wallets require access to the internet and tend to reuse private keys for creating and signing Bitcoin without sufficiently random elements. They are the least secure method, and it should not be trusted with a significant amount of money.

Cold Wallets

A cold wallet moves the funds from online to offline forms, and it is more secure than a hot wallet. There are mainly two popular types of cold wallets in the market: hardware wallets and paper wallets. A hardware wallet is similar to a USB key with no connection to the internet. To operate it, you will need to hook it up to a computer. The best feature of a hardware wallet is that it is impossible for private keys to be leaked from the hardware wallet. Don't forget to back up the seed of the hardware wallet because private keys are derived from it.

Best Practices for Security

In contrast to legacy currency institutions, bitcoin does not have any sort of insurance or regulation against loss. While the relatively lax security requirements of a p2p wallet may be a reasonable trade-off at the retail level, an investment-grade solution, or just a bit more robust p2p option, is called for at the institutional level. Security best practices depend on a thorough understanding of all security factors, plus a clear determination of the risk tolerance and volatility an investor must face in the choice of strategy. While traders tend to employ among the strictest set of security measures - multiple cold wallets, robust p2p wallets for quick payments, secure communications and systems, and analysis of all major forms of hacking - all serious investors should carefully consider the costs and benefits of the best practices.

For example, someone with a relatively modest holding who uses bitcoin only for occasional p2p transactions may find that a publicly available, well-regarded p2p wallet satisfies the majority of their coin security needs - secure storage and public transactions. Alternatively, a large institution that is required to hold a portion of its funds in bitcoin under strict regulatory rules may be willing to make a substantial initial investment to set up a unique and complex mechanism to sign transactions.

The objective of security best practices is to secure your holdings against theft by reducing the exposure to loss, as well as by efficiently managing the risk in using a durable and comprehensive strategy. Best practices will differ depending on individual needs. They will vary depending on the size and nature of risk, the frequency and volume level of transactions, regulatory issues, local risk factors (e.g., asset seizure, or personal risk), and practicalities like access to secure storage.

CHAPTER 8

Cryptocurrency Mining

The SHA256 algorithm is executed in such a way that producing a solution to a hashed block is a cryptographically hard and computationally costly problem. The target solution is adjusted to increase or decrease the frequency of finding a solution to approximately ten minutes. If the target solution is too easy, the block validation process will proceed too rapidly, and the blockchain will grow too fast. The process can also be affected by denial-of-service attacks and generate inflation problems. If the target solution is too hard, it may take too long to validate transactions, and the process could become uneconomical for the network and the cryptocurrency.

Cryptocurrency mining is a process used to secure and validate blocks of transactions by finding a complex solution to a mathematical problem. This process involves validating transactions to get rewards for securing, validating, and adding transactions to the blockchain using specialized hardware that can process the hashes required to find the mathematical solutions to validate a block and complete the proof-of-work required to add the block to the blockchain. The first miner to find the solution for the current block broadcasts the solution to the network. The solution includes a nonce, a string of 32 bits of the previous block, and the cryptographic hash that should be less than a target hash for the block to be accepted by the network.

What is Mining?

Miners have significant economic power and influence over the bitcoin market. They are like the bookkeepers and auditors of the bitcoin network. Originally, bitcoin's protocol rewarded miners with 50 bitcoins, increasingly halved every 210,000 blocks to reduce mining rewards. As of 2018, miners can receive 12.5 bitcoins per block. Miners can also collect "voluntary" transaction fees for every transaction that is included in a mined block. As well as collecting new bitcoin, transaction fees provide a strong economic incentive for miners to include transactions when they mine a new block. Miners play a vital role by allocating computing capacity to hash codes and making the blockchain—and bitcoin network—secure.

Miners are the node operators who create bitcoins by solving complex mathematical problems. Miners ensure that bitcoin transactions are transferred securely into the public blockchain, which provides a tamperproof record of the transfer of the coins. They use sophisticated computer equipment to solve complex cryptographic puzzles. In the process, they help secure the network against false entries and purchase bitcoin transactions. When a miner discovers a "block," he (or she) releases the mined bitcoins. Mining requires both extensive computer power to do the complex calculations and extensive electrical power for the computation. Successful mining can also be considered a way to create new bitcoins and constitutes the primary way that new coins are added to the network.

Mining Methods

Part of mining as an investment concept is that "new money" is created, and is therefore available for investment. The process by which central banks create money was described in section 2.1.1. As that section noted, there are three primary sources of increase to M1 money supply: when central banks put money into circulation; when financial institutions extend new loans to their depositors; and when they invest in non-cash assets. As we also noted, this then gives us three types of potential non-money real asset investments that go straight to the head of the queue, turfing out all the alternative and competing destinations for the cash, so that it can be put to work in their own specific favor. The three types of potential investment beneficiaries are: conventional companies; financial sector-related assets; and inflation hedges like property, commodities, or farmland. However, for this money to be newly created, it needs either to be in circulation outside the banking system or be a deposit in a bank. The important question that cryptocurrencies pose is this: what if the bank guaranteed options for a share of the money, and the financial institution were no one central?

CHAPTER 9

Emerging Trends in Cryptocurrencies

First-generation asset founders like Bitcoin and Ethereum have achieved "development traction," a measure of blockchain platform use that demonstrates the potential for further development and integration of novel second-generation, specialized use digital currencies. While wallets and exchanges that support investing in individual coins can facilitate investment in these easily accessed exchange-listed digital currencies, new innovative financial instruments can capture unique opportunities of new start-up companies and projects that align in vision to interests that cultivate a decentralized future with broader investment approaches.

Greater access and widespread utilization of digital currencies is an example of wealth-building opportunity brought about by the confluence of technology and government policy aims. A wave of new investors and an evolution of the first cryptocurrencies to new generations of digital assets with specialized purposes provides excellent grounds for unique and novel style strategies. Where first-generation strategies focus on coin price speculation, second-generation strategies look for newer financial instruments that might offer enhanced risk and return features with less correlation to Bitcoin's price. These specialized financial instruments include pre-dominance stage private equity in corporations that are using blockchain technology in new and interesting ways, and project debt instruments in specialized cryptocurrency categories already in existence. Specialty representations of general investments like specialized hedging and income strategies will also be covered, as well as refinements of general risk and volatility strategies tailored to meet the unique investor correlation of specialized cryptocurrency investments.

DeFi (Decentralized Finance)
Coming from the very crypto soul and being the real decoration of the virtual environment, DeFi became an innovative application and corrected a lot of crypto misconceptions. Now everyone is able to try investing, not only bank institutions or so-called first-tier investors. In terms of DeFi, a sea of opportunities has opened up. Right after DeFi's introduction, there was a lot of unclear information and an image of an ideal tool for lazy people investing in a pet rock. These views pushed DeFi's actual potential into the background but, fortunately, the situation is rapidly changing and shows us new and fantastic opportunities in just investing money.

If you want to swim with sharks, you have to be brave. If you want to master the cryptocurrency market, you must meet DeFi. The decentralized finance idea has really shaken the market. After the inception, it has shown really outstanding results and made crypto experts acknowledge it as one of crypto's most significant and profitable trends.

NFTs (Non-Fungible Tokens)
It makes it a lot easier to understand NFTs if you see a few examples. Currently, the most common uses of NFTs are: art, music,

virtual real estate, collectibles, and in-game items. All these examples apply to digital products, basically things that can be seen, heard, or played from a screen. Since these are digital projects, they facilitate the NFT trade and transfer. When it comes to real-world items, the advantage of using an NFT isn't apparent since we can't just transfer a physical item at the push of a button. But there are a few areas where the ownership of a physical item could be associated with the token at a certain condition in the future, explained in full the token's features.

NFTs are not a new concept, but they were rather overshadowed by the cryptocurrency world before a recent spike of attention around them. NFT stands for Non-Fungible Token and it means that no two tokens are alike. At first, it might seem that saying that no two tokens are alike isn't that profound. However, when we look at coins, tokens, or dollars, they are the same. Each dollar bill is worth the same, mainly because they have the same print. NFTs are the opposite of that – no two are the same. This feature allows NFTs to serve the purpose of owning something that is unique. This has led to all sorts of new uses and applications of blockchain besides simply transferring access to a certain service (decentralized file storage, generative art, in-game items, virtual real estate, etc).

CBDCs (Central Bank Digital Currencies)

Digital central bank currency: tokenization of cash, replacement of retail banks, destruction of the banking system, instrument of monetary policy in a controlled environment, monetary-financial independence. The fate of central bank money within the completely tokenized world is inevitable, it's just that the process of technological evolution, digital transformation, and operational application will also depend heavily on the perception and urgency of society. For the first time in history, the general public has the opportunity to start a popular discussion of the basic laws regarding the existence and management of money. And it has a scheduled appointment to address its central banker in 2020. With the advent of the first Central Bank's e-euro, society can re-establish the link between work and income, reduce the progressive worsening of inequality, and recover control of the primary tool for protecting individuals and the common good in a liquid and rapidly tokenized world. It would be an unforgivable mistake for Europe not to grasp this historic opportunity.

Today, Denmark, Sweden, Norway, Canada, and Uruguay started testing the use of digital currencies in real-world scenarios - a marked difference from the theoretical road maps of central banks. Time is ticking. The first currency to renew itself; to upskill; to take advantage of all the benefits of artificial intelligence (predictions, optimizations, and self-regulation) already present in society; the first productive asset to become a self-sustainable organization; the first alloy of man and machine to become operational. Money, which must continue to fulfill the four fundamental functions listed above, must renew itself and become a cryptomonetary unit. Every kind of value in the world cannot fail to become increasingly digital.

CHAPTER 10

The Future of Cryptocurrencies

We should remember that our best solutions are sometimes extremely simple and should not be discarded because they show an unneeded complexity. As individuals, we should always strive to maintain full control of our funds, and individuals should not be forced to depend on a trusted intermediary to act as a custodian. Although we can expect intermediaries to participate in the cryptocurrency payment systems, I expect the victory of cryptocurrency and all the applications it enables will be driven by the characteristics described throughout this book. Allowing users to remain in control and benefit from the fundamental cryptocurrency and its remarkable efficiency characteristics.

The day will soon come when cryptocurrency is as simple and easy to use as often as it is to take money from an ATM. The widespread use of cryptocurrency systems should ensure that it will be used for most purposes, not because they are widely available, but because they will bring enormous efficiency into many different aspects of our lives. To ensure that occurs, we should actively support cryptocurrency, and we should welcome its use in all these applications. Although it sometimes has a complex look, sometimes referred to challenging security, balances, network connections, and global conspiracies, cryptocurrency remains the simplest payment system available to anyone. To ensure its effectiveness and reliability, we should continue to maintain its decentralized nature and we should permit competition among differing cryptocurrency payment systems.

Potential Developments
The Crypto Revolution: Investing in the Future of Money
In the tradition of Michael Lewis's Moneyball, The Crypto Revolution makes the next generation of money available to an investing audience, offering new insight into the often misunderstood world of cryptocurrencies.
Potential Developments
In conclusion, the following are some potential future developments in the cryptocurrency space which could propel the crypto revolution forward.
More efficient consensus mechanisms
As PoW and PoS are the most widely used consensus mechanisms, dependent on either processing power or accumulated wealth, the critique attributed to PoW or PoS is that it installs either the rich or the ones that invest a lot of money in hardware in the position of dictators. However, the function of a consensus mechanism is to preserve the supply and protocol.
Widening access to subsidy pools would provide increasingly better options in consensus models. A fair consensus mechanism will give the participants good incentives for strengthening consensus, i.e., the stakeholders should always vote for the winning block. Blocks should be rewarded for the service provided to the maximum number of participants in the network. A high level of consensus

among the stakeholders is essential before introducing revolutionary features to the underlying blockchain technology.

Blockchain will inevitably be one of the enabling tools to meet the challenges for nurturing sustainable, inclusive and trustworthy platforms for production and trade, ultimately creating wealth and prosperity in the 4.0 digital state. As part of the International Trade Centre's World Economic Forum 2018 commitments, the partners are developing a scorecard that can help countries and industries reflect on their readiness to take advantage of blockchain for trade, and refer them to tools and diagnostics to facilitate the design and implementation process.

Challenges and Opportunities

However, every effort to create decentralized digital money had historically been easily squelched by central authorities. This was in part because of a lack of necessity, in part because of skepticism about the technical viability of such projects, and in considerable part because the added protection and palatability of centrally managed digital money tended to satisfy the marketplace. After all, in the 1990s, the vast majority of e-commerce was conducted via credit card, not by digital cash. But much has changed since that earlier time. Technology has improved, while some of the revealed limitations of that monetary construct have ominously suggested its eventual obsolescence.

We spent much of this chapter surveying the forces that are conspiring to birth a general-purpose, non-sovereign, cryptographic money. The emergence of a decentralized, digital, more global form of micro, peer-to-peer money may seem inevitable in a world increasingly reliant on pre-encoded, MacLeodized fiat money. Notions of digital money are probably almost as old as the first computer itself. Moreover, the first government-issued, gold-linked digital money appeared in the early 1980s, with the emergence of debit cards and automated teller machines in Australia, which was the first country to formally phase out its last remaining currency controls. Beyond these antecedents, the attributes of Bitcoin's "pseudo-anonymous" creator, Satoshi Nakamoto, suggest that only then was the idea of a "pure digital cash" tooled to remain truly decentralized and free from the control and counterfeiting that has traditionally accompanied centrally issuing central bank monopolies.

CHAPTER 11

Conclusion

The revolution of Bitcoin is one of property owner control. As we move forward into the digital age, where we will all escape to the cloud, choose freedom with us and invest in the future of money. Not only the future, but also the revolutionary past. Consider allocating a small portion of your diversified portfolio to Bitcoin and the broader crypto-asset space. In understanding that change includes destruction, that it hurts, and that it creates uncertainty, we can coordinate a response in order to minimize the immediate human costs. There are stark implications of these technologies for personal security, freedom of speech, and free association. The future of money is a future of power, for billions of oppressed people all around the world. The silver bullet claimed by happy central planners is a false promise. Only the inherent security, the robustness, and the censorship-resistant nature of the Bitcoin standard can provide a future of increased freedom from oppression. It is our future, and for the first time in many centuries, we have a choice in the interests of collaboration, forgiveness, and compassion are best served by understanding and embracing this tremendous opportunity.

Bitcoin and blockchain technology confront some of the largest challenges that humans have ever faced, and the size of these challenges leads some to dismiss them as impossible. We have all been the beneficiaries of both conscious and unconscious coordination problems and have much to lose if the money and capital that undergird these systems falter.

www.ingramcontent.com/pod-product-compliance
Lightning Source LLC
LaVergne TN
LVHW092101060526
838201LV00047B/1502